# Full Horizon

# Full Horizon

Bruce McEver

*Best wishes.*
*K*
*April 2006*

Jeanne Duval Editions ⊞ Atlanta, Georgia ⊞ 2005

Library of Congress Cataloging-in-Publication Data
McEver, Bruce
Full Horizon / Bruce McEver
ISBN 0-9727455-0-5 (paper)

Jeanne Duval Editions
201-C 5th St. NE
Atlanta, Georgia 30308

Cover and interior design: Meredith Miller
Cover photograph: Oleg March
Cover painting: *River, Early Spring, Soft Light*, 1995, by Margo Trout
Biography photograph: Oleg March
Printed in the U.S.A.

Special thanks to Steve Isaacson of Isaacson Associates
for pulling it all together.

# Contents

# Acknowledgements

This book has been a long time coming, probably thirty years since I first started taking workshops at the New School in New York City. My poems are written between running an investment banking firm and long airplane trips or vacations. I was lucky to take a workshop at the 92$^{nd}$ Street Y with Thomas Lux, who befriended me, encouraged me, and edited this work. I am grateful for Tom's patience and persistence with my work and for his introduction to and publication of this book.

Many of these poems in one form or another have been read, edited, and commented on by a circle of poets and writers associated with my workshops or the summer writing programs at Sarah Lawrence College: Mary Cornish, Stuart Dischell, Ron Egatz, and Kevin Pilkington. I thank them for their helpful suggestions, comments, and encouragement. "Wish You Were Here," "Ma Mora," "A Little Liaison," and "Richmond" were published in *Westview*. "Dark River" appeared in *The Chatthoochee Review*. "By November," appeared in the *Connecticut River Review*. "Horus" was published in *The Cortland Review*, "How Things Never Change" in the *Berkshire Review*, "Snow Geese" in the *Atlanta Review*, and "On the Road" appeared in *Ploughshares*. *Silent Spectacle*, an illustrated portfolio of these selected poems, was produced by Professor Susan Roberts and her students at the Lamar Dodd School of Art at the University of Georgia.

I am also grateful to Margo Trout, a gifted Berkshire landscape painter and friend whose 1995 painting, *River, Early Spring, Soft Light*, graces the cover. It is an honor for this book to revive Tom Lux's Jeanne Duval Editions.

# Introduction

It is not an anomaly now, nor has it been historically, that poets exist outside the halls of academe. In fact, it's only been over the past half century or so that it's become common for poets and fiction writers to earn the bulk of their living as teachers, usually at colleges and universities. In my capacity as a teacher of poetry—the reading and writing of it—I have met dozens and dozens of people who love and live for reading and writing poetry, or for whom it is an essential part of their being, who earn their livings in professions such as business, architecture, law, and medicine. I swear: I've had so many doctors as students that I could turn to one, if needed, as a specialist in practically any body part! Flaubert said that inside every lawyer there is the wreck of a poet. In my experience, there are some lawyers whose poems are sailing high seas, quite well, thank you. I have also had students who are circus clowns, carpenters, exterminators, etc., even some who have been, well, bums. And, of course, I've had many students who were on the way to becoming all of the above and more. Bruce McEver, whose person and whose poems I have known for about 15 years, is a businessman, an investment banker, highly successful, and travels all over the world to do his work. Wherever he goes, poetry goes with him. I've always gotten the feeling, from the lucid and rich imagery of his poems, that poetry was not an escape from his day job (which he loves), but simply his private job, his spiritual job, his night job. There is grief in this book in the form of elegies to his wife Georgia. There is also great joy in this book, celebrations of the business we all have of walking around on earth. There is history and sly humor, different countries and different Americas, but most of all, there is a whole heart in these poems, a heart in the service of a keen eye and ear, the whole heart of a grown man singing, singing with every cell in his body, singing the world alive.

*—Thomas Lux*

# Dedication

*For Georgia Nunnally Johnson McEver, 1947-2000,*
*who taught me to sing*

# I. On the Road

# My Silent Partner

vacations with me best.
He's up for the early profits
of sunrise, golden over tropical
mountains. He delights
in jungle ruins, sad
for the secrets of their tumbled stones.
He's curious about exotic leaf and bird
and prefers verandah reading,
while I tennis with the ladies.
He's quiet at the cocktail hour,
not mixing, but moody by a window,
absorbed and gnostic in sunset.
In these things he is stubborn
and will go on being so
when I am gone.

# Flying

The first star burns
in the western sky, bright
over the fading aurora
that was today:

a navigation beacon
emitting from the shadow zone
of ultraviolet space
that is tonight.

Above the weather's patch quilt
and the just-bejeweling,
spore-like cities, we fly, safe
up here
in my father's place,

where he worked and watched
this continental cyclorama
of earth, cloud, and sky
for all those years,
but never told me.

Tonight I, too, see
the same silent spectacle,
spread a full horizon,
up here
in my father's place.

# Angels from the Realms of Glory

On the Great House veranda,
Tryall's servants' choir performs carols
in black trousers or skirts and white blouses,
before the upright. Their proud
black faces in exultation entertain
the resort's vacationing clans,
dressed in their formal sports attire
(without socks) to celebrate
the advent of the nativity
and to pass along some
tradition to their squirming
and sunburned offspring.

At mass the next morning,
in a scrubbed-white chapel in Hopewell,
the Bishop of Kingston
says we shouldn't let social or economic status
come between us. He's hallelujahed
by a flower-hatted and satin-robed choir
singing to a calypso beat.

Our congregation is so moved
we hold hands and sing another chorus, reaching
across the history of the slave trade:
the burned rum mill ruins
and golf course machete massacre.
We are reminded by His Holiness
that the heavenly host
delivered the good news
not first to kings,
but to poor shepherds
who, tending their flocks by night,
knew nothing
from glory.

# Ma Mora

*for Wallace Lanahan*


A bunch of lazy buzzards gyre
jasmine Jamaican sky.
They've been hanging out up there since sunrise,
after draping their wings to catch first rays
from Ma Mora's tiki roof.

This is Wallace's hilltop heaven
built around an azure pool with a view
commanding Tryall's greens
and sand traps to Montego Bay.
His gardener, John, machete-trims
the bougainvillea
while cook Joyce, strings pole beans
outside the kitchen door
humming a gospel tune.

Her mango-stuffed chicken roasts
for Ma Mora's renters returning from a day of golf.
David, the butler, sets the dinner table
and fusses napkins into birds of paradise.
Wallace loves this place
bought for a tropic gambit
when black tie was *de rigueur*
for drinks at the Great House.

He keeps a watercolor of it
over his bed in Ruxton and awakens confused,
thinking he can see his beautiful wife Betty
on the 10<sup>th</sup> tee overlooking the blue-green bay.
There, in a bobbing red dugout
an old lobster man, toothless now,
but steeled, lean as a rail,
checks his traps

and still brings his fish Fridays
to ask after Mr. Lan-ham.

# Dublin's Doors

are curiously painted
green and blue, red and yellow,
lime and navy, blood and saffron,
along respectable row-house rows
walling drab winter streets,
silently protesting
their stiff Georgian collars,
open for decades
to fill the city's bookstores
with the same sorry story: a fist-fighting

red-head
without much work,
sore at arrogant Anglican overlords,
takes a long pub crawl
and afterwards says the rosary
for brothers and sisters
before emigrating to a new land
to start all over,
determined
and piss-poor.

# St. Paul's Dome

lords over low sooty sandstone flats,
packed to the Thames bounding
the griffin-guarded city
on the winter eve of my visit.
Wren wanted his cathedral to rise, a marble phoenix,
from the ashes of the Great Fire
and center the New London.
Like a gigantic bared breast
of an ancient Amazon,
it dominates the skyline
of glass towers and old church spires.

Interviewing a Market minister,
I hear a man living for his pension.
Job security smothers his domain
like the slow choke of the coal-smoked sky.
Outside his steel-cased windows,
the basilica's crown seems
the only bold and creative idea on the horizon.

Sir Christopher's vision
seems lost in gothic zoning laws,
perfected by a bureaucracy
which thrives behind high iron fences,
making progress like rush hour traffic, queued-up
in boxy black taxis along ancient Roman
and Anglo-Saxon roads named Barbican,
Eastcheap, and Houndsditch.

At my next appointment, the Dome is framed
by a pinstriped banker's carved window.
Backed by ancestral portraits, he's convinced
that real estate is the only hedge
against a falling pound.

He can do nothing about his country's slow slide
into socialism, secure only in his knowledge
nothing will ever change here,
but the guards.

# Forward Brave Heart

Carved over eroded red stone arches
of Castle Drumlanring are odd
little crowned and winged
valentines, crest

for Clan Douglas
who built this stronghold
at the end of a lane of limes:
a delusional peace befalls this valley,
grazed by sheep with nursing lambs
and shaggy red Ayshire cattle
content in the shade of gnarled oaks
as thick and aged as the manor.

Sir James Douglas was knighted
by Robert the Bruce
after the battle of Bannockburn
where, against all odds, the Scots mauled
King Edward's heavy cavalry
and were free.

On his deathbed, King Bruce's last wish
was for his heart to be cut out
and carried by his nobles to the Holy Land.
Like an Aztec priest, Sir James
bore his master's silver-casketed
heart on the Crusade.

When, in pitched battle in Spain,
the knights of the cross were overwhelmed
by infidel slaughter,
the mortally-wounded Sir James
hurled the Heart
into the scimitar frenzy
yowling: *Forward, Brave Heart!*

# The Clearances

I stand on a bare cobblestone beach
watching the ocher kelp heave
on cold waves off the Mull of Kintyre.

Where are the people
who once collected this kelp
for fertilizer to coax
potatoes from these fields,
fields they squared off with rock walls
that march like soldiers
across the moors, along their roads,
around their hovels?

Cairn for the vanished clans
who were finally crushed
by the redcoats at Culloden.
Clanspeople, whose new Anglican overlords,
needing more land for sheep and sport,
cleared them out of their highland homes,
burned the heath and heather
so their shaggy red cattle starved.
Anything to get them off the land.

Remnants of clans came down to this shore,
huddled around their betrayed chieftains
to gather kelp to earn enough for passage.
Here my ancestors waited for the ships
to come out of the Firth of Clyde
from Glasgow and Liverpool,
bound for Halifax, Brisbane, and Savannah,
sowing, far from these desperate reaches,
Scotland's bitter thistle seeds.

# Rhodes

*The immense and moving spirit*
*shall quicken and control.*
*Living he was the land*
*and dead his soul shall be her soul.*

—Rudyard Kipling


Our tour of Capetown comes to his neo-Grecian
mausoleum on the side of Table Mountain,
grazed by zebra and wildebeest,
under still umbrellas and wind-sculptured pines.

Rhodes seized, with his private army,
a million square miles of Africa,
once known as Rhodesia and dined
with Queen Victoria. He died
in 1902, only forty-five.
Our tour guide doesn't know much more about him
but makes some reference
to scholarships.

Slumbering bronze lions,
guarding the temple's steps, view a vast plain
of civilization spread around white compounds. Below
is the last, safe harbor before the Horn of Africa.

He arrived from England,
a vicar's sickly son of seventeen,
to farm cotton with his brother,
who left him for the glitter
of diamonds at the New Rush Mine
in Kimberly. Later, he got the gold fever
at Witwatersand.

Young Cecil followed
and turned these rank speculations
into the De Beers empire
and Consolidated Goldfields.
He controlled the world's diamond trade,
but made more money in gold.

# The House by the Straightened River

has the boy's yard preserved
behind a rusted iron fence: a weathered
doghouse, a tin-topped shed saving
a red canoe, an uneven ladder leading
to a fort up an old apple tree
that spills blossoms this morning like snow
over his white-haired mother
hanging out Monday's wash.

Imagine the boy's life by this river:
fishing when he wanted, romping with his dog,
chasing the geese and mallards
that still strut the green even-sloping banks,
speckled with daisy and dandelions.

And from that fort he watched engineers
change the life of the river
and berm board-straight its errant banks,
clearing a vista now framed with lindens
to the onion-domed spires: the center and symbol of Munich.

Before the war, his father would canoe
summer nights up the river to drink with the Brown Shirts
in the *Bierhalls*. When dad was at the front,
his son would sneak out to the fort and watch
the allied bombers vectoring
the same course.

At the university, after the war, he drank
with his fellow students in those *Bierhalls*
and would drift home on the Isar
in his canoe, crooning of *Gemutlichkeit*,
past mute swans in the gloam
of summer evenings in these high latitudes.

Penniless after his dissertation,
he took a civil engineer's offer
and went to South America to build
petrochemical plants,
joining the ranks of those
who would straighten rivers.

# The Procession of Saxon Electors[1]

Strolling Dresden on an embryo spring morning,
mounds of blackened rubble mind
our raid. The city's baroque genius
that turned sandstone block into nymph,
saint, and satyr is sorted
and pieced back together
like a giant jigsaw puzzle.

Refinished wedding-cake statuary
crowns Augustus the Strong's
palace, jousting court, and orangery
with a stony gaze and simper.
He fathered 365 children and imprisoned
his alchemist, Bottenger, who produced
porcelain instead of gold, fathering
the city's renowned industry.

Our tour ends at a 25,000-tile mural
featuring the city's electors
mounted in historic procession,
prancing to Saxon court.
Here, souvenir sellers hawk postcards
of the baroque extravaganza
that was this city...and under

their tables sell pictures
of the still-smoldering body piles.
That February night
we rained all of our firestormpower
on the German army retreating from the Russian front
incinerating the city and cremating
two hundred thousand citizens
who were heaped
before this yellowed-porcelain wall

with its prancing princes—all that remains
of eight hundred years of history.

# Cathedral

I love to walk the ancient city
with its towers arrayed
against a setting sun and drift of high cirrus.
On weather vanes, lions, dragons
and gilded crosses, face south,
resplendent in last light.

A chilly wind belittles
my jacket before the massive door
to the bishop's seat. I part
the curtain into the sanctuary
where many candles burn. A waft
of wax pervades
the vaulted space.

Worshipers and hushed visitors mingle.
I choose a pew
to listen to the rehearsing choir;
a child's soprano notes
echo over stone arches.

I try to imagine being a citizen
at its consecration five centuries ago,
awed by the sacred stories
luminous in the stained glass and blessed
by their light, seeing the holy
spear that pierced His side and relics
of the Magi in golden cases,
beholding the Master Builder's plan
complete, and my father's and grandfather's all
consuming work done.

Outside, I pass Sunday strollers
dressed in western denims,

admiring buttresses and gargoyles.
We rustle through linden leaves
littering the churchyard,
unable to fathom
when great faith
was last in fashion.

# A Little Liaison

A failing moon rises between the twin spires
of a ghostly Cologne cathedral
that looms over the old Roman city on the Rhine,
spires like great spaceships that never got home.

I meet the wife of an old friend
at a nearby cafe.
She is with a date
who's brought her flowers
and an obsequious grin.

She tells me her husband's
enterprise struggles in the East.
He spends too much time there.
She tennises at ten,
there's a new apartment in Nice,
a new Mercedes, and yes...her new friend.

I remember their wedding day in Paris,
an incredibly handsome pair.
I remember, too, their first child
pinned in a blue blanket
to contain him while daddy
ran a smelter in Tennessee.

I excuse myself early
and walk a damp stone-inlaid street
of antique dealers
who sell without sin the freshly unearthed
shards of their Roman past.

Like little European affairs
and those twin gothic spires
that took six hundred years to build,
we blacken
with our burning of coal.

# Wish You Were Here

Your first view of the Alps
stepping from the clean Swiss train
proclaims arrival at the very gates of heaven.

Sublime steeples and *stupas*,
the birth pangs from aeons of geological agony,
command the clouds.
In summer's sun their snow fields and glaciers perspire
spilling a chalky-blue melt
over falls and down cobbled streams.

On a slope below the timberline,
a tanned, gaunt farmer and his wife
turn hay with big-toothed rakes;
their cattle and goats, secure with collar bells,
graze high pastures.

In the village, chalets with geranium boxes
under every window welcome all.
Remember when we were first here
and tried our stumbling student-German
on a friendly innkeeper?
She took one look
and offered us a room
for a couple of hours!

Recall the mountains,
nestled under the *decke*,
like angels
bathing bare-breasted
with their sisters
back at the *Frauenbad*
by the *Zurichsee*.

# City Planning

Nothing seems out of place
at Philly's Four Seasons Hotel
where Vivaldi backgrounds
briefcase-bearing ladies and men
meeting for breakfasts of yogurt and buns.

Outside, early traffic encircles
Logan Square centered around Calder's
bronze fountain memorializing the city's three rivers:
an Indian woman, warrior, and maid recline nude
for morning commuters under spewing water
from the mouths of turtles, fish, and swans.

The Square's central to the Franklin Parkway
laid out to echo the *Champs-Élysées*,
and the principles of classic city design,
with beaux-arts circles spacing
a boulevard of linden, leading
to a crowning pantheon.

The city designer, William Penn,
saw municipal quadrants centered
around squares of civic purpose.
What would the founding father think today
of his site designed for the burial ground and gallows
as a homeless trio splashes in the summer spray
with those nude bronzes honoring
the Delaware, the Wissahickon,
and the Schuylkill?

# Richmond

Undeterred by over a century
of industrial progress since the War,
the cold, stone-cobbled James
runs through Richmond's heart.

The river floods the brick-clutter relics
of old cannon foundries, tumbled tobacco
warehouses, wracked bridges, dams, and locks.
Now, on its banks, modern towers taint pink
toward sunset and shadow columned porticos.

It's charming and everywhere:

I negotiate with a landed banker whose family
financed the Cause or chat
with an ex-Marine cabby back to the airport.
His great-granddaddy dug and manned
those earthworks surrounding and strong-holding
this sacred capital.

It even seems alive in the glimmering eyes
of the great generals' oils arrayed
at the Commonwealth Club. J.E.B. Stuart,
Stonewall, and Lee,
whose stares of determination and damnation
glow and secretly ember
in the bosom of the citizenry,

that courteous,
soft-spoken Southern character,
somewhat deceptive,
but capable of taking on vastly
superior forces
and sometimes
whipping them.

# The Falls of the Mississippi

At Minneapolis the Corps of Engineers managed
to collar in a cement straitjacket
the river's sandstone cliffs where the Blackfeet believed
the Great Spirit once lived.
They crossed the falls with arched bridges,
cut a canal through them with locks, and muffled
or did away with any mist or roar.

Along the river's bluffs,
hulls of old flour mills
that made this town's first money,
await renovation into hotels or demolition.
Glass towers defining the modern city
are linked by a skyway maze
that fills with the hearty workforce,
on those cold-snap winter days.
The buildings have begun to lose
their local owners to distant mergers.

Like the one with the family's name on it,
where I worked, after a rogue trader crippled it.
They agonized over how to rescue the franchise
their grandfather started. A big bank showed up,
making it easier to take a profit
than save a tradition.

At the bottom of the muffled falls
the great river begins
its 2500 mile course to sea
with a mad, muddy boil.

# On the Road

I love early mornings in a new hotel,
traveling west and up on east coast time,
before room service starts delivery,
searching the lobby or even down in the kitchen for coffee,
to greet dawn with the night clerk
starting his wake-up calls.
I find a paper from the bundle by the revolving door
and a town map from the tourist's rack
to discover where I am and what's happening,
having missed the previous day, sequestered
with clients in a windowless conference room.

I hardly notice a busboy picking up
last night's glasses and emptying ashtrays
to start the lobby over with a worn smile by seven.
I begin to feel oddly comfortable
before the stir of day,
unhurried and almost at home
in the contrived elegance
of overstuffed couches, old marble, and mirrors.

I wonder how much of my life
has been spent, just like my father's,
in rented rooms and strange beds
with our precious time
neatly folded and packed
into suitcases and carried
between the unforgiving schedules
of people and planes?

## II.  Harness Tightening

# Harness Tightening Time

We walk the worn red dirt road ruts
to the rusted tin-topped barn,
lichened green-gray,
and almost overgrown
    into the woodland's edge.

We begin to unravel the honeysuckle
scenting and tangling the tumbled paddock.
With a sputtering chain saw
we clear the pine, sweet gum
    and sassafras saplings

whose bleeding rings count
seven springs
since David sold the buckboard
and turned his back
    on fooling with horses.

On May afternoons like this
we'd coax the horses out of their shade
down by the creek with sweet feed.
Dave would hitch Sonny to the surrey
and we'd saddle Sixten and Syllabub
and he would guide us beaus
    around Little Sandy Farm.

Jokes, saved for our visit,
were the first order of business
and we'd pass the family burying plot
where your great grandfather's leg –
lost during the civil war –
    lies buried beside him.

When we got to news from the big city,
we were by the old family house
with its shanty foundations out back.
Here your Grandmother was born
and officiated the brewing of syllabub[2]
    Christmases.

At five o'clock sharp we'd stop
at Double Bridges across the Little Sandy.
The red dust cloud would settle
and into the well-stocked cooler,
carried like a treasure chest,
we'd dig for "a harness tightener,"
    as Dave termed it.

Your mom, now widowed,
pays the bills here
and plays her piano,
mistress of her solitude
on her family's farm worn
    from two centuries of cotton.

You taught me to ride
in this paddock on a day like today.
Sonny's, Sixten's,
and Syllabub's spirits
live here now,
because you say
they always return
    to where they're happiest.

And one fine afternoon
maybe we will all return
to Little Sandy
for harness tightening time.

# Queenie

When my father got his first job flying
after the Pacific War we moved
into a basement apartment
close to the Atlanta airport. There
I came into my first memories:
the small rust-brick house had a steep driveway,
high holly hedges, and out back,
an iris garden tended
by our landlady, Mrs. B.

My knees were always skinned careening
down that driveway on my little wheeled
black and white pinto horse named Queenie.

Then, in Eisenhower's recession,
they furloughed my father.
He found a job as a bill collector;
my mother cried at the kitchen table,
not wanting to go back to teaching.

Worse, I got sick, with a fever
I couldn't shake and a bloody cough.
The doctor's prognosis: *bronchial pneumonia,*
*get him out of that damn damp apartment,*
but we didn't have the money for it.

I remember the gurgling vaporizer,
mom lovingly spreading smelly Vick's VapoRub
on my chest and those horrid sleepless nights, sweating,
seeing demons in the shadows of my nightlight,
coughing myself into exhaustion.

I longed to ride Queenie,
just get out of that place, even visit the doctor.

Then spring came and the fever was gone.
My mom and Mrs. B. held my hands,
walking the iris garden in full bloom.
It smelled...azure heaven.

Dad got rehired to fly short late-night runs
to Charlotte, Shreveport, and Baton Rouge.
He didn't care where
as long as he was flying.

# Unfinished Business

*For my father, Harold Bell McEver*
*July 29, 1920–December 16, 1996*

You find your way back
to that mausoleum wall, the only space
without plastic poinsettias in this cemetery.
It has snowed in Atlanta

and the mum and gladiola sprays
that blanketed his casket sprawl
in a frozen and blackening pile
where the workers tossed them,
their spoiled ribbons rustling.

When you first saw
his mortuary-made up face
from the casket, it was a shock,
but everyone managed a nice word.
You never before rode in the car
saved for the most bereaved
behind the hearse.

His pilot friends, their breaths frosting
like a well-trained draft team,
carried the casket here. It took two preachers
and a bishop to bury him
and shut the marble door.
There was no earth to throw.

This morning's solace
is a lone swan
floating in a half-iced pond,
the only thing alive
to take your full confession.

# Graduation

A mocking bird twitters
unnoticed in the slash
pine shading the light-robed graduates
marching across center stage.
They balance the mortarboards
like books on their heads
and toss their tassels.

Navigating
the phalanx of black robed
faculty convened
before the Doric pillars
of the red brick school,
each name
read is a striding
achievement.

The admiring assembly
of fathers, mothers, sisters, and uncles
cry, clap, squirm, and fan,
polite and perspiring,
through a spring morning
without a breeze
as we go through the alphabet
one last time
together....

# Manhattan Morning

It is in the early hour,
as first light pinks
the apartment canyons,
when Gotham stirs and stretches.

Then confusion's messenger
is easily dispatched,
my thoughts let go
of the traffic din and all
fades to background.

Sadness passes,
and I come close
to something huge and still,
like this city after a heavy snow,
silent, yet alive....

# Spring Rain

Cold drops pock pothole pools
along New York's roadways.
Traffic grinds slow to work,
horns cry for resolution, needing
to get on with things
organized around money and time.

It's near the end of the flowering
when the Japanese Cherries in the park burst
into white and pink clouds over greening lawns.
This is only an attraction
for the bees who are...all about honey.

In spring, nature's agenda
is clear: on this damp morning I run
a bridle path littered
with petals like confetti
after the big game, spilled in the rush
to green.

# Horus

City birdwatchers bunch, binocular-eyed,
at the rim of the model boat basin
to watch a reluctant red-tailed
hawk fledge from a nest high over Fifth Avenue.
At first, the nestling tries
a tenuous flutter, then he dives
and soars into a feathered crossbow.

Son of Osiris and Isis,
the falcon-faced god of light's
effigy crowns Central Park's obelisk
erected in 1600 BC in Heliopolis
and given by Egypt
to the City of New York in 1906.

At home, I rip
open mail with a silver horus-headed blade
bought in a Cairo *souk*
and read about
Rameses' coronation
and the assembled court's astonishment
when a falcon dove out of the sun
to land on the prince's shoulder.

*The hieroglyph translation*
*on the obelisk reads:*
*The Horus, Strong-Bull...*
*King of Upper and Lower Egypt*
*Chosen-of-Ra, the Golden Horus*
*mighty-in-years and great-of-victories,*
*Son of Ra, Rameses, Beloved of Aten*
*who came forth from the womb*
*to receive the crowns of Ra,*
*Lord of Two Lands.*

On a clear, storm-scrubbed
morning after a run, I stretch
under the obelisk, watching
Horus incarnate rip
the guts from a plump
city pigeon atop
the Met's roof-garden pavilion,
screaming the sheer whistle,
annunciation
of the god's
return.

# III.  A Place by Water

# Dark River

In memory of
Georgia Nunnally Johnson McEver
January 20, 1947–December 24, 2000


It was winter, like now.
We searched long for a place by water.
The first night in our unfurnished house
we lay in a sleeping bag
joyful on plain pine boards.

Through sunrise's haze,
we overlooked the river
defining the valley.
It wound south
between bare tree-lined banks
fresh with snow.

You said the river had moods,
would change color with each season
and it did: olive springs,
summer's green, and amber falls.
It took all the sorrow
from highland people to the sea.

Four days past
the solstice the river steals
down its confines
to where the sun sinks
red on the horizon.

For me, it will not rise again.
Ice floes scrape and spin
blown by raw wind,
pieces of a cold puzzle
freezing this river over.

Out of clear dusk,
Venus rises, so bright
I could climb
that gloam-etched tree,
and pluck her from the sky.

I cannot fathom
this early darkness, my love...
I want to go away,
anywhere, till the river changes
colors. But I stay

here, where we were going
to grow old
together.

# Fallen Flowers

I

At 4:00am, under Diamondhead's
worn molar, my light is an orphan
on this high-rise reef
ringing Waikiki.
I tend a little memorial
on my dresser next to a candle: your toy
lamb and yellow beach bonnet,
the hotel's welcome lei, a heart-shaped
box of candy, and a photo
of us with friends in the country
and our pet goat.

All's quiet now at Hale Koe,
the house of warriors,
as far away as I could go to heal.
The large orange and yellow carp
feather in the lobby pond beneath lotus pads.
The soft breeze motions
the air-borne roots of the central banyan
like pendulums recounting time
and rustles palms like dancer's hips
weary of the hula.

Later, provisioning at the PX,
I see a skin-headed ensign
and his sunburned bride pushing
a shopping cart full of pans and paper towels.
They're a portrait of us thirty years ago, before
I sailed for Southeast Asia.
Setting up household like my dad and mom, before
he flew to the Pacific war.

II
I climb to the Punchbowl,
a necropolis of our fallen
in an extinct volcano crater
overlooking Honolulu.
On its north rim, the first were buried here
as columns of oily smoke rose
from the battleships still burning in Pearl Harbor.

Over a hundred manicured acres,
smooth-barked banyans shade
the remains from each avenging step
across the Pacific to a setting sun:
Midway, Guadalcanal,
Rabaul, Coral Sea,
Bougainville, Leyte Gulf,
Surigao Straight, Saipan,
and Mt. Suribachi.

Reviewing the long march of crosses,
the multitude of markers decorated
with Valentine flowers strikes me.
My father's fallen comrades initiate
me into that left-behind legion
who ration out sorrow's petals.

III
The Jains believe only fallen flowers
are suitable for worship.
At first light, I walk the hotel gardens
gathering wind-trimmed flowers
for your memorial. I take back fresh
tropical fragrances and bright colors:
purple, azure, and saffron.

Not bad
for my second day

on the job.
I have some coffee and wonder
what the maid thinks.

# Refuge

I
The ancient Hawaiian's revered
places of refuge like this black lava flat
at Honaunau Bay.
It's staked with some straggly palms and crossed
by a pumice block wall divvying
the refuge, or *pu'uhonua,*
from the thatched-roofed royal
compound by the king's landing lagoon,
occasioned by sea turtles.

A park ranger in breechcloth
coolly weaves a mat of palm leaves
telling the story of his ancestors:
Polynesian Vikings,
who followed a great shark
and the luminous constellations,
of these latitudes.
They crossed hundreds of ocean miles
in hand-hewn outrigger canoes
full of breadfruit, pigs, and dogs,
searching for new islands,
and a place of refuge.

Here, the condemned or those who
had stepped on the king's shadow,[3]
meaning instant death,
could be saved and granted absolution.
if...they could make it
to this place.

II
On the road back to Kona,
I visit the Old Painted Church.

Guarded by a friendly dog,
the white wooden-latticed chapel
and its necropolis, dug
from rust-red volcanic slope,
overlooks the azure bay.

The interior is a shoebox Sistine
giving the illusion of St. Peter's
with columns of palm trees.
Inside, whispering tourists wander,
snapping cameras.

I pick a pew next to a mural
of St. Francis' epiphany.
After a day of dragging grief
around, I prostrate myself.
Sobbing overtakes me.
It happened so suddenly,

did I step on God's shadow?
I imagine Jesus comes
down from his cross
and offers me an orchid lei.
There's breathing next to me,

a cold nose on my thigh,
then a paw on my knee,
and a motor-tailed mutt
gives me
an absolution lick!

# Line Dance Heaven,

a bright blue banner
in a Honolulu shopping mall, proclaims.
A western fling where
Asian ladies in cowboy boots
and hats step, clap, turn, and sway.

Center stage, in turquoise tassels,
their leader croons
to the twangy tunes.
Held Wednesday's at seven,
this is a widow's stomp.

The single male is an Hawaiian
under a Stetson, attending
his lover drooling
in a wheelchair near the DJ.
Rejoining the ladies' lines,
he causes a twitter,
a *bodhisattva*
with a blue bandana.

Clomp, turn, step, clap, kick
and turn with your departed beloved.
They're urns of ashes
under black marble markers
on the volcano's slope…or
on my shelf back home.

Forget your loneliness.
Remember, the scroll of surf,
warm sand sifting through your toes,
smooching, yes…and palm-framed
sunsets on Waikiki
just down the street.

Nice postcard, cowgirls!
I can join your club.
Get in line and face
the music.

# The Vision

I

High cirrus dimmed Christmas Eve's sky.
Isabel went to pray for an ailing friend
at the old quay out on the Hudson
and was aghast to find her sitting
on a bench in a white fur coat
facing the half-iced river and the mist-
draped mountains beyond.

II

Isabel's car slalomed up the steep drive,
straightened and bumped along
the ploughed furrow to the cabin,
where we bereaved gathered.
Missing the memorial,
she and her son came in to offer tea
and small talk until the boy said:
*Tell them.*

III

Isabel's story was strange
because my wife had a white Russian mink coat,
bought on a birthday whim.
My wife named the coat Natasha.
One night, wearing it, she enticed me
to skate with her on a black-ice lake.
She pirouetted like a polar bear,
spotlighted by passing cars.
Under Natasha, she wrapped herself, chilled and sick
after chemo, in our window seat,
smelling of the treatments.
I pretended not to notice.

IV
Two months later, I followed Isabel west
through bare orchards yearning for spring.
Church spires, spiritual watchtowers
of these little towns, hold
their necropolises close.

V
*It's here,* Isabel said, as I turned
the car onto the snow-powdered path.
Her dog Brandy, following fresh deer tracks,
led us down to the river beneath
her great grandfather's home, Olana.

*It was a day like today, about the same*
*time in the afternoon,* she remarked, not knowing
it was the same time my wife died
or that we came to Olana to toast
sunsets on special occasions.
I chilled, recalling the painting of it
hanging above my wife's piano.

We pilgrimed, silent, afraid our footsteps
crunching snow would frighten the spirit
waiting at the end of the dock.
The wrecked pack-ice
piled up around the quay,
a hard-edged tribute to the simple bench
of cinder block and bleached board,
sided by cedar and thorns: heaven's gate.

*So, what did you say?* I asked.
*There were no words spoken,*
Isabel whispered. *There was, instead,*
*a complete understanding*
*that something horrible happened;*

*then the deep peace shared between us*
*assured me she was all right.*
*There was an emerald glow*
*around her head,*
*and when she turned toward me,*

*there was no face.*

## Snow Geese

Sometimes there were signs.
After the March maelstrom,
I snow-shoed up
our mountain in morning sun
and tracked into another storm.

At first, I thought the yappings
were coyotes chasing me.
But vee-ing overhead,
all white with black-tipped wings,
calling me...then disappearing
into the oncoming blow,
was a flight of snow geese.

By the time I got down,
the cottoned forest was prismed
in the thawing light. Drops glistened
and draped every tree
like a diamond necklace
adorning my wife,
singing *The Merry Widow.*

For a moment,
Vilia was in the mist
between tall pines.
The wood nymph's presence
was fresh and chilly,
a rush of rivulets....

Winter loosened its grip—
like the last clutch
of my wife's hand before she slipped
into unconsciousness.

# Candle

*Why suffer in darkness*
*when you can light a candle?*

—Chinese proverb

A clairvoyant told me:
*She's still with you—*
*light a candle,*
*call her in,*
*ask for a sign.*

What power
for a simple string,
a wick in wax,
to transcend worlds.

So, I light my candle
morning and evening.
It has become sunrise and sunset.

Care must be taken
with this precious light.
I once left mine burning,
and when I returned,
a battery-dead pencil sharpener
was grinding away.

Now, when I see candles glowing
in a church, I am full
of respect for those called-up spirits.

Think about it,
meditate on the flame.
Feel its heat
and energy.

It takes you back
to the light
from where you came.

# Memorial Day

Morning sun spotlights
*Monroe Memorial Park*
in white wrought iron arching
over a field of lichened tombstones
quarried nearby.

The yard is full of fresh flowers today
and the old rustling plastic ones
as well as small star-and-bar
battle flags waving by Confederate tombs.
There's your Great-Great Uncle's statue
facing South toward his farm, standing erect
as he died with his sash and broken-off sword,
leading this county's infantry
the day his rebels crested
at Gettysburg.
Strange to be here without you.

Your grandmother rests
under that crepe myrtle, and there's a grassy spot
by David for your mom.
At last night's family reunion
on her farm, I felt like an amputee
returning from the war. Your relatives ask:
How are you holding up?

Well, I'm partial
to walking through dew-wet cemeteries
where I can openly cry.
I shovel my sadness
like grave diggers who mound
the fresh red clay on canvas and cover
it with astro-turf for an afternoon service.

We left-behinds tend tombstones
and our urns, bring the flowers and flags,
nod to one another, biting
our lips to reconcile ourselves
before these old gray warriors.
Facing your loss
is their price for admission.

# *Advent 2001*

The moon slices through bare branches of old oaks,
mum Druids of Charlotte suburbs.
Christmas lights outline manor hedges,
boxwoods scenting of stability.

Defiant stars and stripes drape every house.
This year we've learned the crescent
marks the end of Ramadan
as well as the start of Advent.
The peace prince has more work.

I walk a sidewalk buckled by the oaks
downtown where bank towers,
the city's cathedrals of commerce,
dominate the skyline.
They loom silver at dusk,
ghostly erections conjuring
ancient San Gimignano.[4]

It is near the anniversary of my wife's death
and the world has changed:
Many grieve and question
the wisdom of tall towers.
I saw them burn.
When I go back to my empty room,
progress is not crying.
I light a candle;
it's all I can do.

# IV. Hawk Rise

# The Swans at Golden's Bridge

Those elegant white hooks slide by, sustained
on their long lake
along Metro-North's Harlem Valley line.

Through the perpetually
filthy commuter-car panes,
I search for my
totems.

Hello, my mystic friends:
pen and cob,
floating on your half-iced
waters.

You are Friday's first salutation
and Monday's aesthetic
farewell.

# Utopia Farm

When lilacs scented
Housatonic hedges
we walked from our weekend cabin
to the old boys' camp next door.
We wrestled this from a failed developer
who planned a subdivision
of country estates to be named
the Blackberry River Run.

Touring our abandoned camp
after the closing, past
the boarded and tumbled cabins,
the months of haggling pay off
with a periwinkle ground cover
in azure profusion.

You're dressed in a red checked shirt,
faded jeans, and tattered straw hat.
Our path cuts across an overgrown field:
we talk of horses pasturing there,
renovating stalls in the old barn,
and building a pond edging the wetlands,
sourcing the stream meandering the meadow.

This is so distant from the city
where we could barely pay
the rent when we started.
You were singing late nights and weekends,
and I was traveling week days
and working spreadsheets the rest.

In a seed-heavy sea of green,
high before the first haying,
flaked purple-white with fleabane

and yellow with buttercup and hawkweed,
we leave a wake
of trampled grass across our prairie,
the dew soaking
our trouser bottoms.

Indians camped at the fork of these rivers
and settlers left stone footprints
of cabin cellars and walls across the acreage.
They knew this alluvial land was rich,
the forests full of cedar and ash for fence and rail,
straight white pines for barn sides
and oaks for stall interstices.
From our hillside, an artesian well gushes
that watered the camp and filled a pool
where 120 butt-naked little boys
bathed summer mornings!

It is strange we should settle
here…under Canaan mountain,
in Weatogue valley,
so far from our native places,
seeds scattered,
but now sown,
taking root,
feeling home.

## The Kid

The horses' heads follow
my path to the big barn door
as I check on the baby saanen
we saved from the meat market.
He shivers in pain
in his pen, his long ears drooping.

He got clipped yesterday,
tripping behind me like Pan
to the appointed place.
He was too small
to anesthetize.

His uncle, a goat of great girth,
butts him away from the first food
the kid tries to nibble.

Poor thing hobbles
from me, flashing his purple
iodized back side,
shunning the one who held him
while the vet
squeezed and cut.

# Hardwired

Two shots break the gloam: and the extended-cab
Ram races away.
We drop our drinks
and run to the overgrown field
where a white-tail
struggles,
unable to stand, shot
through the spine.
Her twin fawns flee.
Eli fetches the neighbor's gun
and finishes the botchery.

The doe's eyes are open black pools
as we drag her limp body to the road
and await the game warden.
We seethe,
our hate hardwired.

# *Anger*

comes up like a tropical afternoon thunderstorm
blown dark over the mountains,
a sudden shower spilling
and crashing like a closet of pots.
An outburst, wetting sun deck and windward windowsills,
throws errant thunderbolts,
scattering foursome, foreman and crew,
dampening the best of parties and plans,
and leaving feelings in its wake
like muddy rain-pocked ponds
running into raw
rocky gullies.

# *January*

is the shush of snow
falling across bare field and wood,
redefining outlines
of fence and bough by white.

It is early dark evenings
huddled around a hearth
divining the coals' glow.
It is burrowing under layers of blankets
when night winds wail
like coyotes running deer,
bad as any bad dream.

And before morning's graying,
it is the secure rumble
of the town's plow, scoring the rural road
through a shower of sparks
and a whirling wake of white.
It is a cold, penetrating sun-up
and snow that keeps

falling…like the recurring dream
of the one alive last fall,
who makes no breath now,
even in this frigid air, nor
leaves a shadow
as easy as bare maple branches,
oddly blue, on winter's blank page,
but bids you:
*be still.*

# March

is the reluctant month when winter wanes
over Canaan mountain
and the ice shelf looses its grip,
breaking up to glide
a melt-swollen river.

Frozen footprints are mud
by midday, but errant
cold rains and snow keep
overcoats reserved on the peg.

The days are longer when the vernal equinox is crossed,
sure and impersonal as multiplication tables
and, somewhere in the Yucatan,
the feathered serpent's shadow slides down
the great pyramid.

Here, first bulb's fingers seek sun,
the sap buckets are set,
willow branches quicken and bronze,
and in the thawed swamp,
a primordial chorus of spring peepers start.

While on that gray mountain,
a bear, hungry from hibernation,
crawls from a rocky crevice,
comes to terms with the bright morning,
and gets on
with finding his breakfast.

# Near Canaan

*Death is a debt to nature due.*
*I've paid mine and so must you.*

—Old Connecticut tombstone

The news is inconvenient for you tonight,
just settled in on vacation,
knowing something back home's gone bad wrong.
The doctors can't explain the water on his lungs,
and your sister calls saying his kidneys are malfunctioning...
On his 70$^{th}$ last month,
you took a long walk together, but he tired,
leaving things still unfinished between you.

August heat haze hangs
tonight like soft fog so
you can barely see Orion's belt, east of Taurus,
or sleep right, feeling sticky and uneasy.
You're late awake
listening, through a concert
of incessant cicada,
to a distant semi downshifting
and an epiphany of three angelic chimes
from Canaan Episcopal's new carillon.

Our tabby, Princess Di, returns
with a half-eaten mole, having worked the wood lot all night,
and wants in, scratching on the screen door,
and through the haze
you hear the old shade's whisper: *nature's due,*
*nature's due.*

# October's

yellow flares of sugar maples
parade against slate-gray cloud bottoms
riding over the rusting countryside.

It's a morning of frost
and the steaming river Housatonic.

It's plump pumpkins, oranging
farmer Howden's fields under the Taconic range.

It's the smell of ash and oak logs split
and stacked for snow.

It's the first hearth-fire
and piles of burning leaves
on Canaan's lawns and sidewalks.

It's the musk of a woods walk,
ankle deep in its stripped colors.

It's black lazy buzzards
catching a late morning thermal
over stubble-cut corn fields.

It's ghost and goblins and jack-o-lanterns.
The month we costume to celebrate the day of the dead.

It's the sun just up
to start another day's chromatic show

and the clear morning sky checked with gangly vees
of Canadian geese honking,
spread across a full horizon.

# By November,

the Berkshire's leaves have rusted away,
molding on forest floors,
in gutters, or scattered
across small town sidewalks.
Yellow flares of aspen stand
on mountain sides and gold triangles
of tamarack in the marshes,
fall's last banners.

On this raw rainy morning
you hate the thought of facing winter square,
knowing it's five full months
before you change the snowtires
or put away your heavy herringbone coat.

You take courage watching a farmer slog
through muck and manure,
galoshed and going about his chores,
and realize the routine you hide behind
when prospects get grim.

There's inspiration in fall's last color dash.
You slow down on the way to the crumbling
Dover Plains commuter station
and try to remember why you are going there.
Is it good for you,
like saying your prayers?

# December's

about hope endowing evergreens.
Cedar, pine, spruce
trees and wreaths
smell sap-sticky
and remind us of a forest
despite the office party's din.

Evergreens stand watch
beside New England graveyards,
and their sprigs are buried with the Masonic dead;
under them we spread the season's bounty
and cradle the holy creche.

Boughs hold stars
on winter solstice nights,
and those lights are echoed
in triangles in town squares across the county,
in homes throughout the world,
in pairs up Park Avenue,
and in a grandee contributed
each year for Rockefeller Center.

The one I like best
is the little one in front of our home
that greets us with tiny twinkling lights
at the end of our long drive to the country
where we are up Christmas morning squinting
into the golden spotlight of a low-angled sun
over snow-loaded evergreen boughs,
the temperature below zero,
and the cold-start replay
of miraculous birth.

# How Things Never Change

In a hieroglyphed wooden box
stiff miniature men wearing white kilts and sandals
sit tending tiny exquisitely
carved black and white cows,
just like the Holsteins

along the Housatonic
at the Shady Maple Farm,
manned by my mustached neighbor, John
and his suspendered crew,
who know all about cows
and slog galoshed
through mud and manure,
spreading its abundance on their fields.
They work on unending chores for their cows,
somehow making ends meet
until the day they drop.

Like their ancient brothers
who tended Metuhotep's herds by the Nile,
four thousand years ago,
they travel together,
an eternal memory, $ka^5$
from the Middle Kingdom.

# Blue Smoke

I. China
The knowledge of iron-making
came to China on the backs of shaggy camels
whose masters traded silk
for its secrets with the Assyrians.
By the sixth century BC, the jade-handled swords
of the Hans drew more blood.
Iron-tipped plows behind yoked oxen
started a farming revolution celebrated
each spring equinox by a furrow plowed
by the emperor
at the Temple of Heaven.

It took one thousand years
for the plow and yoke idea to get back west.
Nothing's changed since 119 BC, when the emperor Wu Ti
declared a monopoly on iron smelting
(and later added liquor).
Today the Communists also plant trees on the equinox
to replace those cut down by ancestors
for cities and charcoal.

Our tour bus navigates the coal haze
through the sprawl of Shanghai
to China's largest steel works, the Baoshan
on the Yangtze. Sporting yellow hard hats,
we begin at the raw material pier
where dinosaur-size shovels take 15-ton hematite bites
from the *Cape Hawk's* holds.

Central to the complex: three blast furnaces
fed crushed ore and coke
refined from mountains of dusty coal.
The crucibles' melt spills into ingots and blooms,
feed stock for rolling mills.

We walk a skyway over glowing slabs kneaded
and squeezed by gigantic rollers
through the steam, smoke, and fury
of a computerized vulcan from Germany
whose goal is rolls of sheet metal in minutes.

On the skywalk, the heat is face-felt
from smoldering metal rolls waiting
to be stamped into cars, washers, and tin cans
for over a billion Chinese,
awakening from dusty villages and slums,
needing a modern diet of steel.

II. Connecticut
Road ruts and tumbled stonework
of those who toiled before us are the most visible earth-scars
on forest floors in puny winters:
the remains of waterwheel-powered enterprises
cut by bucksaws and hauled by ox boat
when suspenders really held up your pants.

The first time I saw one of the circular mounds,
I feared Indians were buried in my back yard,
but the town forester allowed it was the work of colliers
whose charcoal circles covered this countryside
by the end of the last century.

These men, among the best-paid iron mill hands,
cleared the earth circles in the woods,
stacking up to fifty cords in tight mounds
then covering them with leaves and mud to slow
the burn, airless, to carbon.

If this process worked right,
after seven to ten days, the smoldering
mound blew blue smoke;
on the other hand, too much air

produced ash and white smoke,
flame-burst, or worse, an explosion.

It was the slow burn to blue smoke
that once hazed and deforested this valley.
Like log locusts for each blast furnace,
colliers cleared five square miles of woodlands
a year to keep them burning and belching.

Charged around the clock
with plentiful charcoal, local limestone, and iron ore,
dumped through the top-gorging arches,
thirty crucibles breathed the hot air blast
from bellows turned by waterwheels
along the Housatonic and Blackberry Rivers
until they emptied the Salisbury ore body.

Our Revolutionary and Civil Wars
and America's wakening West
were poured from this melt of progress.
In a hundred years
trees grow back,
open pit mines fill to lakes,
furnaces turn to piles of stone
marked by historical plaques next to swift rivers,
their slag heaps grow headdresses of birch,
and industry moves on,
leaving rusted pieces of barbwire
grown halfway
through old oaks.

# Hawk Rise

I bike into a Sunday bathed
in bright light flooding the Housatonic.
Slate-bottomed clouds bearing autumn
drift from the west into the clear sky
cathedral spread over the Taconic Range.

At Shady Maple Farm
I greet my neighbor
astride his tractor, harvesting
his dry-tasseled corn field.
Crossing the river's bridge,
I watch his cattle graze and grace
the pasture along its banks as irregular
as their black and white hides.

Like the cloud's shadow,
today I wander free
over this valley floor. I run
the broad meadow, yellowed in goldenrod,
and climb to the foothill forest, tinged
early red. I cross a field dotted
orange with pumpkins, linger
at flaxen haystacks,
left like giant bread loaves
in an emerald bed.

My thoughts reach
for the mountain tops,
their new energy like the wind
traced in the rusting trees.
Something released, silent, and then soaring
with that harbinger hawk
rising, spirit's messenger
over this green, green field.

# Footnotes

1. Electors were German princes entitled to elect the Emperor of the Holy Roman Empire.

2. A sweetened drink or topping made of milk or cream beaten with applejack brandy.

3. The ancient Hawaiians believed the king's shadow was his essence or *kapu*; it was death to tread on it.

4. A Renaissance Italian city-state where rival families built ever-taller towers.

5. The ancient Egyptians believed *ka* was the spiritual duplicate of a person that after death traveled back and forth between the land of the living and the land of the dead.

**Bruce McEver** was raised in Atlanta, Georgia, where he attended Woodward Academy and graduated from the Georgia Institute of Technology. He was an exchange student at the Technische Hochschule in Hanover, Germany, and received an MBA from Harvard Business School. He is an investment banker and the Chairman of Berkshire Capital Securities LLC, a firm he founded in 1983.

Bruce started writing in workshops in New York City with Hugh Seidman, Pearl London, Katha Pollitt, Brooks Haxton, David Lehman, and J.D. McClatchy. He has taken writing seminars at Sarah Lawrence College with Thomas Lux and Kevin Pilkington and, most recently, was a summer residency student at the M.F.A. Program for Writers at Warren Wilson College, where he worked with Stephen Dobyns. His poems have appeared in *Ploughshares, Westview, The Berkshire Review, The Cortland Review, The Connecticut River Review, The Chattahoochee Review* and *The Atlanta Review.* He works in New York City and lives in Salisbury, Connecticut on Utopia Farm.